TOKYOPOP® SNEAKS™

Introduction

Welcome to the latest installment of TOKYOPOP Sneaks, your insider's guide to the wild and wonderful world of manga!

As you may already know, manga – the Japanese word for comics– has become a truly global phenomenon. All over the world, readers can't get enough of its irresistible visual storytelling and bleeding-edge graphic design. There's manga for every taste, too: science fiction, romance, comedy, fantasy, action...you name it and TOKYOPOP has it covered!

Within the pages of this book, you will find an extraordinary selection of TOKYOPOP's latest titles that are sure to fire your imagination like nothing you have ever read before. Once you pick out your favorites, remember that TOKYOPOP manga is available everywhere books are sold.

Check your local bookstore or go to your favorite e-commerce site to buy the latest and greatest TOKYOPOP manga.

From all of us here at TOKYOPOP, thank you for your support – and welcome to the Manga Revolution!

TABLE OF CONTENTS

Ark Angels

The Story:

Shem, Ham, and Japheth are siblings from another world. Equipped with their magical powers and a fantastic whale-shaped ark, they are charged with saving all the creatures of Earth from becoming extinct. When they aren't saving our world from destruction, these young people live like normal humans: they go to school, work at a flower shop, hang around with friends and even fall in love. However, someone or something sinister is trying to stop them...

The Creator:

Sang-Sun Park

Behind the Manga:

•From the creator of TOKYOPOP's bestselling Tarot Café

FANTASY

T

TEEN
AGE 13+

SRP:

£6.99

{Chapter 1}

YAAAAAAAA!

Our first expedition starts today.

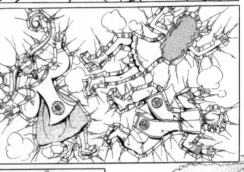

This is Hamu. She likes to complain.

Damn! My hair is all messed up!

OWWWCH... YOU REALLY NEED TO WORK ON YOUR LANDINGS!

She is my second-oldest sister. She got the good looks, but was made disagreeable in return. She hates men with a passion.

11

Mariana Archipelago
Guam

THE YEAR
IS 1968.
THE PLACE IS
GUAM'S MARIANA
ARCHIPELAGO.
OUR QUARRY IS THE
GUAM FRUIT BAT.
OUR WINDOW OF
OPPORTUNITY IS 24
HOURS!

I was the one who explained it...

I thought you were here to capture me...

...but then again, someone as beautiful as you can capture me any time she wants.

CHU

WHERE DO YOU GET OFF KISSING ME?! YOU'RE JUST A BAT!

WATCH IT MISTER!

OOPS. HEH-HEH... ANYWAY, WE SHOULD GET OUT OF HERE.

MARK OF THE SUCCUBUS

BY ASHLY RAITI & IRENE FLORES

Maeve, a succubus-in-training, is sent to the human world to learn how to hone her skills of seduction. But things get complicated when she sets her sights on Aiden, a smart but unmotivated student at her new high school. Meanwhile, the Demon World has sent a spy to make sure Maeve doesn't step out of line. And between Aiden's witchy girlfriend, his nutty best friend, and Demon World conspiracies, Maeve is going to be lucky to make it out of our world alive!

Here is a Gothic romantic fantasy set in one of the most menacing worlds known to humans: high school.

T TEEN AGE 13+

FOR MORE INFORMATION VISIT: WWW.TOKYOPOP.COM

The Story:

Not every lost soul is a lost cause.

When a young girl moves to the forgotten town of Bizenghast, she uncovers a terrifying collection of lost souls that leads her to the brink of insanity. One thing becomes painfully clear: The residents of Bizenghast are just dying to come home.

A finalist in TOKYOPOP's Rising Stars of Manga™ competition, Marty LeGrow has crafted an unforgettable Gothic drama that will leave readers haunted long after the last page is turned. Visit LeGrow's website: www.bizenghast.com.

The Creator:

M. Alice LeGrow

Behind the Manga:

•Selected for Teen People's HOT LIST in 2005
•"LeGrow's artwork is nothing short of stunning." — IGN.com

FANTASY

T
TEEN
AGE 13+

SRP:

£6.99

20

21

I JUST DON'T KNOW, DOCTOR. I DON'T LIKE THAT BOY COMING HERE TO SEE DINAH, BUT SHE THROWS HERSELF INTO HYSTERICS IF HE'S KEPT AWAY. WHATEVER SHE'S SEEING SEEMS TO GO AWAY WHEN HE'S AROUND.

THE LOSS OF HER PARENTS SO EARLY IN LIFE CONTRIBUTES TO HER DELUSIONS. THIS PARANOIA OF GHOSTS AND GOBLINS MIGHT TURN INTO *REAL* SELF-HARM ONE OF THESE DAYS. YOU SHOULD REGULARLY CHECK HER FOR MORE SCRATCHES OR BITE MARKS.

WE MIGHT HAVE TO MOVE HER TO THE HOSPITAL IN WATERTOWN.

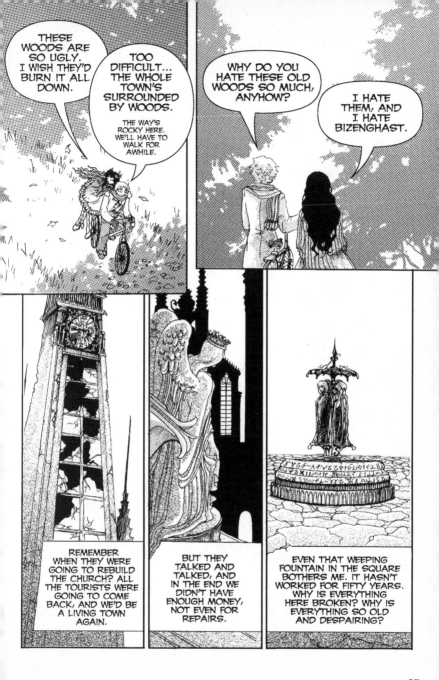

THESE WOODS ARE SO UGLY. I WISH THEY'D BURN IT ALL DOWN.

TOO DIFFICULT... THE WHOLE TOWN'S SURROUNDED BY WOODS.

THE WAY'S ROCKY HERE. WE'LL HAVE TO WALK FOR AWHILE.

WHY DO YOU HATE THESE OLD WOODS SO MUCH, ANYHOW?

I HATE THEM, AND I HATE BIZENGHAST.

REMEMBER WHEN THEY WERE GOING TO REBUILD THE CHURCH? ALL THE TOURISTS WERE GOING TO COME BACK, AND WE'D BE A LIVING TOWN AGAIN.

BUT THEY TALKED AND TALKED, AND IN THE END WE DIDN'T HAVE ENOUGH MONEY, NOT EVEN FOR REPAIRS.

EVEN THAT WEEPING FOUNTAIN IN THE SQUARE BOTHERS ME. IT HASN'T WORKED FOR FIFTY YEARS. WHY IS EVERYTHING HERE BROKEN? WHY IS EVERYTHING SO OLD AND DESPAIRING?

27

CHRONICLES OF THE CURSED SWORD

The Story:

Rey Yan was an orphan with no home, no skills and no purpose.
But when he discovers the PaSa sword, a cursed blade made from
the bones of the Demon Emperor, he suddenly finds himself with the
power to be a great hero. The sword's creator is the evil Shiyan,
prime minister to the emperor, who needs the sword to assist him
in releasing his ancestor, the Demon Emperor.

The Creator:

Story by: Beop-Ryong Yeo
Art by: Hui-Jin Park

FANTASY

T
TEEN
AGE 13+

SRP:

£6.99

HUFF

HUFF

HUFF

HUFF

WHY NOT SURRENDER NOW, YOUR HIGHNESS?

HUFF

HIS MAJESTY THE EMPEROR DESIRES YOUR HEAD.

clutch

HOW DID...?

HEE HEE HEE, YOUR HIGHNESS. MASTERFUL TECHNIQUE INDEED.

WHAAT?!

HEY MISTER, ARE YOU OKAY THERE?

LITTLE HUMANS, YOU DON'T SEEM TO VALUE YOUR LIVES...

The Story:

In real life, Roto, Boromid and Ah-Dol are average kids with average problems, but in the virtual world of Lost Saga, they're heroes. They might even become legends...if they can stop bickering long enough to level up. Whether it's werewolves running rampant or a gorgeous pair of troublesome thieves, our boys must be ready for anything, because in Lost Saga nothing is what it seems and murder can happen with a click of a mouse.

The Creator:

Story by: Hee-Joon Son
Art by: Youn-Kyung Kim

Behind the Manga:

•From the creator of TOKYPOP's PhD: Phantasy Degree

FANTASY

T
TEEN
AGE 13+

SRP:

£6.99

I HAD TROUBLE LOGGING IN...

TIME IS MONEY, BABY!

THAT'S WHAT I HEAR. DIDN'T I LEND YOU 500 GOLD LAST NIGHT? MAYBE YOU WANT TO PAY UP?

JUST KIDDING! WE JUST GOT HERE, TOO. I'M JUST MESSING WITH YOU.

SO...THIS IS NOMAL CITY? THE CAPITAL OF LUCIFERIA? WHAT A DUMP!

WHAT DID YOU EXPECT?

MAYBE YOU'D RATHER BE BACK IN EZTOWN?

I CAN'T BELIEVE WE WASTED ALL OF LAST NIGHT THERE.

WE WERE ONLY THERE SO LONG BECAUSE SOME IDIOT PRIEST KEPT GETTING US FURTHER AND FURTHER IN DEBT!

WHAT IDIOT PRIEST?

YOU, IDIOT!

OH, RIGHT. WELL, ARE WE GOING TO STAND AROUND ALL NIGHT? LET'S GO FIND SOME ACTION!

TELL ME AGAIN WHY WE HANG OUT WITH HIM?

BECAUSE HE'S GOT THE BAND-AIDS. SOMEONE HAS TO PUT US BACK TOGETHER.

AND IT'S NOT GONNA BE ME. THINK THERE ARE ANY DUNGEONS AROUND HERE?

BEATS ME. WE SHOULD GET A MAP. DID YOU SEE ANY SHOPS?

ROTO?

ROTO NO MOVE.

WHAT'S GOING ON BACK THERE? ARE YOU TWO MAKING OUT AGAIN? GROSS!

YOU HIGH-PING BASTARD, ARE YOU FROZEN AGAIN?! WHEN ARE YOU GOING TO SPRING FOR A DECENT CONNECTION?

THAT'S THE THIRD TIME THIS WEEK...

......!

HELLLLLOOOO, ROTO! ANYONE IN THERE?!

WELL, I GUESS I'M OFF THE HOOK THEN! THANKS, ROTO!

IF YOU WANT ME TO PAY YOU YOUR MONEY BACK, SAY SOMETHING NOW!!

BOROMID, I THINK HE'S...

48

I'M IN.

BUT...

WHY DO I ALWAYS SPAWN IN A BATHROOM? I WONDER IF THAT PATCH KWAN-SU GAVE ME...

HUH?

YOU'VE GOT MAIL!

Sender: Ah-Dol
Did you force quit? We'll wait for you in the tavern. Don't take all night.

Reply_   Delete_

THANKS A LOT, AH-DOL...

WHICH TAVERN? YOU IDIOT...

LOOK, IF I'M NOT REALLY HERE, AND I'M NOT REALLY DRINKING, THEN WHAT'S IT MATTER WHAT I'M NOT REALLY DRINKING?

LOOK, THAT'S JUST THE WAY IT IS!

THEY PROBABLY FIGURE THAT IF WE GET USED TO DRINKING IN THE GAME, WHEN WE TURN 21...

...WE'LL START SPENDING OUR TIME HANGING AROUND IN BARS INSTEAD OF PLAYING COMPUTER GAMES. NOW SHUT UP AND DRINK YOUR SASSAFRAS.

SNIFF!

IT'S JUST NOT FAIR! OFFLINE I'M NOT WALKING AROUND KILLING MONSTERS, AM I? SO WHO CARES IF I DO SOMETHING DOWN HERE I CAN'T DO IN THE REAL WORLD?

HUH?

IT'S JANG-GUN. LOOKS LIKE HE GOT BACK IN.

HMPH! FINALLY.

Roto: Hey, Woon-suk! How am I supposed to know which tavern you're at?

THE GUARD PROBABLY PULLED HIM IN FOR BEING OUT PAST HIS BEDTIME!

DO YOU THINK THEY HAVE A "LOST CHILD CLAIM" HERE, LIKE AT THE MALL?

SERIOUSLY, HE LOOKS LIKE HE'S ABOUT NINE!

PITA-TEN ™

By Koge-Donbo - Creator of Digicharat

The girl next door is
bringing a touch of heaven
to the neighborhood.

Fruits Basket

Life in the Sohma household can be a real zoo.

The Story:

Amanda is a lonely little girl. Her mother means well, but doesn't have a lot of time for a 9-year-old and, after plenty of begging from Amanda, agrees to let her have a pet. Amanda chooses a ferret (and names her Peach) because ferrets aren't ordinary and, darn it, neither is she! But her mom sets up Two Big Rules: 1) Amanda has to care for Peach, and 2) Peach can't ever bite Amanda. It seems like Amanda finally has the friend she's needed...but Peach sees Amanda's hands as five-serpent monsters--and bites in what she thinks of as self-defense! What will little, lonely Amanda do if her mom finds out her new best pet is actually a biter?!

The Creator:

Jared Hodges & Lindsay Cibos

COMEDY

ALL AGES

SRP:

$6.99

The Perfect HOUSEPET!

clink
clink
clink

TARANTULA ON SALE!

O-OKAY SWEETIE!

ANYTHING WOULD BE BETTER THAN THIS GUY...

THOSE THINGS?

WELL.....

SIT TIGHT WHILE I ASK THE CLERK ABOUT THEM.

OKAY!

COME HERE, LITTLE FERRETS!

WARNING!!
we bite!

CReek

WICK.

WICK

REACH...

WHO WANTS TO COME HOME WITH MEEEEE...?

CHOMP!

chew chew

64

65

EVIL NEVER DIES...
BUT EVIL STUFF DOES!

FROM THE
WINNERS OF
TOKYOPOP'S FIRST
RISING STARS OF
MANGA™
COMPETITION

PHANTASY DEGREE

The Story:

Sang is a fearlessly spunky young girl in search of the Demon School Hades. Fortunately for her, she comes across a group of misfit monsters that are ditching class from the Demon school. She convinces them to sneak her into the class that normally only allows monsters to attend. Mystery, intrigue and high jinks unfold as Sang finds a way to become a monster--and begins a fantastic adventure in a devilish domain!

The Creator:

Hee-Joon Son

Behind the Manga:

•From the writer of TOKYPOP's iD_eNTITY

FANTASY

T
TEEN
AGE 13+

SRP:

£6.99

I'M **SOOOO** HUNGRY THAT I DON'T HAVE **ANY** STRENGTH TO MOVE.

BUT THERE'S JUST ONE TINY PROBLEM.

PLOP

SLUMP

WHAT A BARREN WASTELAND! I CAN'T FIND A SCRAP OF FOOD **ANYWHERE**.

groan

pant pant

WHAT'S THIS? A LITTLE DOGGIE...?

STARTLED

THAT'S NO DOG! IT'S A WEREWOLF!!

EEEEEK!!

Hmmm... He's not technically human, so it wouldn't really be like cannibalism...

WAG WAG

GRIN

His meat might be a bit stringy, but it's gotta be chock-full of nutrients!!

???

pant

YELP!

RUB RUB

HEY, NOTHING PERSONAL, FURBALL. I HAVE TO EAT TO SURVIVE, TOO, YA KNOW...

GLIMMER TWINKLE

WHAT DOES IT *LOOK* LIKE I'M DOING? I'M PREPARING DINNER.

WHAT DO YOU THINK YOU'RE DOING?

ISN'T IT MAKING YOUR MOUTH WATER?

CERTAINLY.

BUT I THINK I WANT TO PUT *SOMETHING ELSE* ON THE MENU!

This can't be good.

AH-WOOOOO!

I'LL TAKE THAT AS A YES.

AWW, WHATEVER. I ADMIRE YOUR DEVIL-MAY-CARE ATTITUDE!

SO, C'MON, SHOW ME YOUR SCHOOL!

HOW-HOW DID YOU GET LOOSE?

WELL... I DON'T *REALLY* MIND BEING TIED UP ALL *THAT* MUCH...

You just didn't tie it very tight...

쿡쩍

AMAZING! THOSE KNOTS WERE ESCAPE-PROOF!

YOU WANT *US* TO GIVE *YOU* A TOUR OF HADES? DON'T BE RIDICU-LOUS.

DO YOU ACTUALLY THINK A *HUMAN* WOULD EVEN GET PAST OUR SCHOOL'S *FRONT DOOR?*

scratch

I SUPPOSE YOU HAVE A POINT.

OH! I HAVE AN IDEA!

THE DRAGON HUNT Is On...

WARCRAFT®
THE SUNWELL TRILOGY™

RICHARD A. KNAAK · KIM JAE-HWAN

From the artist of the
best-selling *King of Hell* series!

It's an epic quest to save the entire High Elven Kingdom from the forces of the Undead Scourge! Set in the mystical world of Azeroth, *Warcraft: The Sunwell Trilogy* chronicles the adventures of Kalec, a blue dragon who has taken human form to escape deadly forces, and Anveena, a beautiful young maiden with a mysterious power.

EXPERIENCE THE MANGA

T
TEEN
AGE 13+

The Story:

In the not-too-distant future, sovereign nations have been replaced by corporate city-states. War is entertainment-- scheduled, televised and rated. It's the new opiate of the masses and its stars are the elite Psychic Commandos, known as "Psy-Comms." In the corp-state of Electromedia, no star shines brighter than that of Mark Leit, a young man with the ability to see flashes of the immediate future. Mark was destined to become possibly the greatest Psy-Comm of all time, but a tragedy from his past and a desire for redemption will cause Mark to abandon everything his life has stood for.

The Creator:

Story by: Jason Henderson & Tony Salvaggio
Art by: Shane Granger

Behind the Manga:

•As seen in NEO Magazine!

SCI-FI

T
TEEN
AGE 13+

SRP:

£6.99

WHAM

THANKS.

SURE, ANYTIME.

M-MARK...

RAVEN!
I DIDN'T...
I **COULDN'T**
SEE THIS.
I'M SORRY...

OH,
NO!

95

CHAPTER [2]

Six Years Later.

99

WELL, LET *ME* TELL YOU WHAT'S IN OUR FUTURE, OKAY?

WE'RE GOING TO GET THOSE TWO *GIRLS.* HANG ON--

HERE, LADIES! CALL MY MEDIA GUY. HE'LL SET SOMETHING UP!

BUT...BEFORE WE HOOK UP WITH THEM, WE'VE GOTTA TRY AND STAY *AWAKE* WHILE THE COMMANDER CHEWS US OUT FOR WHATEVER WE'RE SUPPOSED TO HAVE DONE *WRONG* TODAY.

DAMMIT! DAVID, GET DOWN -- DUCK!

FWMP

KRANG

KRANG

KATAKA TAKA

105

107

ELECTROMEDIA CORP IS LYING TO US ALL.

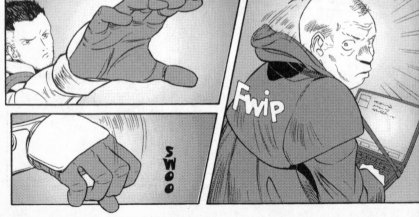

FWIP

SWOO

HEY! YOU TWO! C'MERE!

RUMMBLE

RIP

RIP

AH!

A MIDNIGHT™ OPERA

Immortality, Redemption, and Bittersweet Love...

For nearly a millennium, undead creatures have blended into a Europe driven by religious dogma...

Ein DeLaLune is an underground Goth metal sensation on the Paris music scene, tragic and beautiful. He has the edge on other Goth music powerhouses—he's undead, a fact he's kept hidden for centuries. But his newfound fame might just bring out the very phantoms of his past from whom he has been hiding for centuries, including his powerful brother, Leroux. And if the two don't reconcile, the entire undead nation could rise up from the depths of modern society to lay waste to mankind.

The Story:

Three hundred years ago, the Sorcerer Kalutika Maybus sealed the vampire Deshwitat in limbo after killing his fiancee, Lilith. For centuries, Deshwitat's mind calculated revenge while his body slumbered...until now. A band of spiritual investigators has inadvertently broken the seal that binds Deshwitat, and the vengeful vampire has been released. A lot has changed since the 17th century. Carriages have been replaced by cars, the Internet connects the world, and vampires have become the stuff of legends. But beneath the veneer of technology, magic and religion still reign supreme. Kalutika is the most powerful person in the world, although few actually know he exists. Prophecy foretold that Kalutika would destroy the Earth, so Deshwitat's quest is now not just one of revenge, but of redemption...for himself, and the world. Joined by an excommunicated exorcist and a spiritual investigator, Deshwitat begins his bloodquest. The hunted is now the hunter!

The Creator:

WOO

SRP:

£6.99

TOKYOPOP® SNEAKS™

Introduction

Welcome to the latest installment of TOKYOPOP Sneaks, your insider's guide to the wild and wonderful world of manga!

As you may already know, manga – the Japanese word for comics– has become a truly global phenomenon. All over the world, readers can't get enough of its irresistible visual storytelling and bleeding-edge graphic design. There's manga for every taste, too: science fiction, romance, comedy, fantasy, action...you name it and TOKYOPOP has it covered!

Within the pages of this book, you will find an extraordinary selection of TOKYOPOP's latest titles that are sure to fire your imagination like nothing you have ever read before. Once you pick out your favorites, remember that TOKYOPOP manga is available everywhere books are sold.

Check your local bookstore, go to your favorite e-commerce site, or visit TOKYOPOP's online shop at www.TOKYOPOP.com/shop to buy the latest and greatest TOKYOPOP manga.

From all of us here at TOKYOPOP, thank you for your support – and welcome to the Manga Revolution!

TABLE OF CONTENTS

TOKYOPOP Sneaks UK 2006 vol. 1

Cover Art – Christian Lownds
Graphic Design – Alyson Stetz
Project Coordinators – Josh Pool, Dennis McGuirk and Rob Tokar
Digital Imaging Manager – Chris Buford
Pre-Press Manager – Lucas Rivera
Art Director – Anne Marie Horne
Managing Editor – Lindsey Johnston
VP of Production – Ron Klamert
Editor-in-Chief – Rob Tokar
Publisher – Mike Kiley
President & C.O.O. – John Parker
C.E.O. & Chief Creative Officer – Stuart Levy

A  Manga

TOKYOPOP Inc.
5900 Wilshire Blvd. Suite 2000, Los Angeles, CA 90036
E-mail: info@TOKYOPOP.com
Come visit us online at www.TOKYOPOP.com
http://www.tokyopop.co.uk/

TOKYOPOP® SNEAKS™

RIGHT-TO-LEFT CHEAT SHEET

This book is printed "manga-style," in the authentic Japanese right-to-left format. Since none of the artwork has been flipped or altered, readers get to experience the story just as the creator intended. You've been asking for it, so TOKYOPOP® delivered: authentic, hot-off-the-press, and far more fun!

DIRECTIONS

If this is your first time reading manga-style, here's a quick guide to help you understand how it works.

It's easy... just start in the top right panel and follow the numbers. Have fun, and look for more 100% authentic manga from TOKYOPOP®!

ディアーズ

The Story:

Aliens have landed on Earth and are now a normal part of society. These beautiful beings have been given the name "DearS" and are trusted and welcomed by most humans. In order for the DearS to learn Earth's customs, they are sent to random high schools for "home-stay." When Takeya helps a DearS on the way home from his school, she calls him "Master." Thus begins the humorous life of Takeya and his sexy alien follower, Ren, who tries to figure out the wacky customs of this place called Earth!

The Creator:

Peach-Pit

Behind the Manga:

The manga that inspired the hit anime!

COMEDY

TEEN
AGE 13+

SRP:

$6.99

2nd Contact

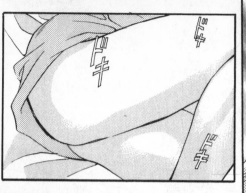

URGH...

· · · · · ·

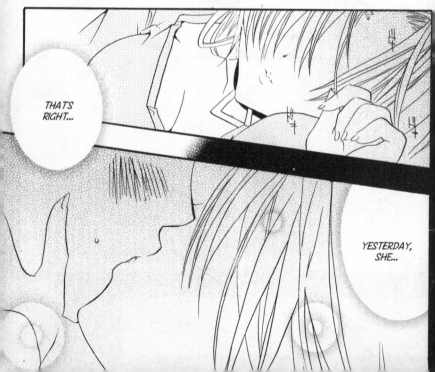

THATS RIGHT...

YESTERDAY, SHE...

WHO...?
WHO IS SHE?

TODAY JUST KICKED MY BUTT.

...

AAAHH...
I'M SO SLEEPY...

HOW COULD I JUST FALL ASLEEP WITH THAT THING IN MY ROOM?

ZZZ ZZZ

. . . .

OH YEAH, THAT'S HOW IT WENT.

ちら

....

LIKE PEARLS BEFORE SWINE.

A GIRL LIKE THIS IN A ROOM LIKE MINE...

SHE'S NOT A GIRL! SHE'S AN ALIEN! AN ALIEN!!

NO NO NO! SNAP OUT OF IT, TAKEYA!

MMM...

WHO KNOWS WHAT EVIL LURKS BENEATH THAT ANGELIC FACE!

LAMENT of the LAMB

SHE CAN PROTECT HER BROTHER FROM THE WORLD.
CAN SHE PROTECT THE WORLD FROM HER BROTHER?
AVAILABLE JUNE 2005

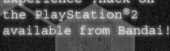

TWILIGHT TALES

The Story:

"All that glitters...even the stars...all things precious... even your life...the King of Bandits can steal it all in the blink of an eye."

Take a fantastical, far-out journey in the out-of-this-world adventures of Jing, the King of Bandits and his feisty, feathered friend Kir! Do not miss the sequel to the fan-favorite Jing: King of Bandits!

The Creator:

Yuichi Kumakura

ACTION

T
TEEN
AGE 13+

SRP:

£6.99

SO...A CITY NAMED RUSTY NAIL, EH...?

YEAH...

PRETTY SAD NAME, HUH? NOTHING LIKE A CITY THAT'S USELESS, YET HARD TO PULL OUT!

THOUGH LATELY, IT HAS FOUND A PURPOSE.. FOR THOSE SEEKING TREASURE.

WELL, IF IT'S A NEST YOU WANT... LOOK UP.

AW, C'MON, JING. MONEY AIN'T ENOUGH. LOVE, MAN—GIVE ME LOVE!!

LOVE STRONG ENOUGH TO MAKE ME WANT TO BUILD A NEST...

19

LOOKS LIKE A NEST FOR THESE GUARDIAN BIRDS THAT LIVE AROUND HERE.

HMM, GUARDIAN BIRD...I LIKE THE SOUND OF THAT!

"HEY BABY...WHY DON'T I BE YOUR **GUARDIAN BIRD** TONIGHT?" HEH HEH!

WAIT—AREN'T WE MOVING **AWAY** FROM THE CITY, JING?

WELL, I AM A BANDIT. THOUGHT I MIGHT TAKE THE **BACK** ENTRANCE FOR ONCE.

BACK ENTRANCE...?

...AND WE'LL END UP AS MORE **TRASH** IN THIS STINKIN' HOLE.

BOOM

CLINK

...BUT TO HIM, IT'S A STATUS SYMBOL!

♪

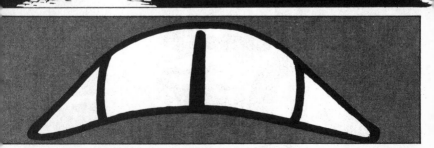

IF I GET HIT BY THAT, I'M FINISHED.

BO

INITIAL **D**

INITIALIZE YOUR DREAMS!

TOKYOPOP®

**Manga and Anime
Now Available!**

www.TOKYOPOP.com

SAIYUKI RELOAD™

The Story:

The sizzling-hot sequel to the hit manga series that topped the charts begins right here!

The fearsome foursome continues their journey west towards Shangri-La, encountering new challenges and new adventures along the way. Their legend precedes them, but not always in the way one might expect. The Minus Wave that apparently drove all the Youkai in the land mad looks like it might have missed one, as Sanzo, Gojyo, Hakkai and Goku meet a lone guardian and the band of children he cares for. Fear and misunderstanding run throughout this particular leg of the journey, even between the members of the Sanzo group!

The Creator:

Kazuya Minekura

Behind the Manga:

• The manga that inspired the hit anime!

SRP:

£6.99

WHOA, MAN.

YOU'RE QUICK.

WHO THE HELL ARE YOU?

WHOO!

EASY, SANZO. HE'S COOL.

CHECK IT OUT.

YOU'RE A PRETTY DANGEROUS PRIEST, AREN'T YA?

THAT'S SOME GREETING.

...YOU...

THE GENTLEMAN SAVED US AFTER OUR FALL.

SO YOU GUYS ARE TRAVELERS, RIGHT?

NO ONE FROM AROUND HERE WOULD HIKE UP THIS FAR WITH CLOTHES AS THIN AS YOURS.

ANYWAY, I'M SORRY.

FOR MY KIDS ATTACKING YOU AND ALL.

KIDS?

SO THOSE--

WHA?

WHOA!

DON'T TELL ME ALL THESE ARE *YOURS*?!

NAH, I'M SINGLE.

APOLOGIZE TO THE NICE MEN, KIDS.

WE'RE SORRY.

WE'RE SORRY!

UH... S-SURE.

......

YEAH.

THEY'RE ALL YOUKAI?

WHEN THE YOUKAI STARTED GOING BERSERK...

...SOME OF THE ADULTS-- BUT MOSTLY THE KIDS-- HELD ONTO THEIR SANITY.

I DON'T KNOW IF IT'S BECAUSE THEY HAVEN'T FULLY MATURED AS YOUKAI OR WHAT.

BUT AROUND THESE PARTS, I'M THE ONLY GROWN-UP LEFT.

THESE KIDS WERE LEFT BEHIND BY THEIR RAMPAGING PARENTS. THEY'RE ORPHANS NOW, IN A WAY.

I GATHERED 'EM ALL TOGETHER AND BROUGHT THEM TO LIVE HERE.

ANYWAY. WE'RE HIDING OUT IN THIS MOUNTAIN TO--

WHAT TH' HECK?!

OW OW OW! GET OFF! DON'T PULL THAT!

GYAAAAAH!

OOH, A TOY MONKEY. I LIKE THAT.

Ha Ha Ha!

ANYTHING ON THE FLOOR'S FAIR GAME FOR PLAYTIME.

YAKI-IMO?*

YAKUMO, ARE THESE PEOPLE GUESTS?

YAKUMO.

*A BAKED POTATO.

YES. THAT'S OUR GOAL, ANYWAY.

HUNH.

SO IF YOU FIND OUT WHO CAUSED THIS, THE YOUKAI WHO WENT CRAZY MIGHT GO BACK TO NORMAL.

YOU'RE LOOKING FOR THE CAUSE OF THE CALAMITY?

WITH ALL THE THINGS THE YOUKAI'VE DONE UNTIL NOW, I'M NOT SURE THE HUMANS WILL FORGIVE THEM.

WHAT DO YOU MEAN?

BUT WOULD THAT REALLY FIX EVERYTHING?

THAT'S A LOT OF FEAR AND DISTRUST TO GET OVER.

IT WON'T BE EASY.

DO SOMETHIN' ABOUT TH' LITTLE CRAZIES!

HEY! OSSAN!*

*USED TO REFER TO MIDDLE-AGED MEN. SHORT FOR OJI-SAN.

HEH HEH. TYKES GOTS TA PLAY WITH OTHER TYKES, Y'KNOW.

GYAAAAAH!

OSSAN, AM I?

KIDS-- THE LOUD ONE SAYS YOU'RE NOT PLAYING HARD ENOUGH.

WHA?

SHUT IT! I GOTTA MAKE NICE TO THE FUTURE HOT LADIES OF THE WORLD!

THAT'S SO LAME! YOU'RE PRETTY POPULAR THERE, GOJYO!

BWA HA HA HA!

...I'M SORRY FOR THE NOISE.

DON'T WORRY ABOUT IT.

BUT YOU YELL WAY LOUDER THAN WE DO!

KEEP IT *DOWN* WHILE WE'RE *CRAMMED* IN HERE, PEA-BRAINS!

46

erica
SAKURAZAWA™

Friends Lovers And Everything In Between

ANGEL · NOTHING BUT LOVING YOU · BETWEEN THE SHEETS
ANGELNEST · THE AROMATIC BITTERS · THE RULES OF LOVE

The Story:

Through a series of misunderstandings, hardworking waitress Fuu, arrogant mercenary Mugen and mysterious samurai Jin find themselves running from officials and wanted by the law. Together, they form an uneasy alliance to search for the enigmatic Sunflower Samurai. Along the way, they find misleading characters, ninjas, assassins and even a prince in disguise. Their journey proves to be nothing less than a roller coaster ride of battles, danger, desperation and companionship!

The Creator:

Story by: manglobe
Art by: Masaru Gotsubo

Behind the Manga:

•Based on the hit anime!

ACTION

TEEN
AGE 13+

SRP:

£6.99

THERE'S NO MIS-TAKE!

...THEN *YOU'RE* MY OPPONENT.

IF YOU WERE SKILLED ENOUGH TO KILL *THEM*...

DO YOU NEED A *REASON* TO KILL SOMEONE?

I think you do...

WHY?

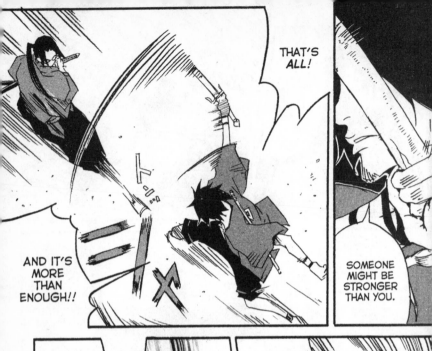

THAT'S *ALL!*

AND IT'S MORE THAN ENOUGH!!

SOMEONE MIGHT BE STRONGER THAN YOU.

AAAAAH!

RIGHT?!

51

THIS IS LIKE NO FIGHTING STYLE I'VE EVER SEEN!

THIS MAN'S MOVEMENTS...

HAH!

THERE'S NOTHING PRACTICED ABOUT THEM.

Why is he just swinging them around like that?

...AND HIS ARMS...

HIS FEET...

...ARE COMPLETELY RANDOM!!

Uh

!!

THAT SAID...

THERE'S FAR TOO MUCH UNNECESSARY MOVEMENT...!

...THIS GUY IS GOOD!!

FINALLY.

YOU UN-SHEATHED YOUR SWORD.

oooo

GREAT! NOW YOU'RE GETTING IT!

WHOA!

...AND I FIND THIS INTERESTING...

FROM THE LOOK OF THINGS, YOU DON'T KNOW THE FIRST THING ABOUT SWORDS-MANSHIP, BUT...

...YOU'RE *VERY* GOOD!!

56

59

www.TOKYOPOP.com

TOKYOPOP®

Suikoden™
幻想水滸伝

A legendary hero.
A war with no future.
An epic for today.

WE INTERRUPT THE MANGA TO BRING YOU THIS VERY IMPORTANT ANNOUNCEMENT:

pause

read right-to-left

If you've been enjoying the unforgettable left-to-right reading experience, we invite you to jump to the back of our book for more cutting-edge manga...this time from Japan!

read left-to-right

If you've just soaked up the hottest manga from Japan, you need to turn to the front of our book for some of TOKYOPOP's originally created manga and other cool articles.

Of course, if you're blown away by what you've been reading, then e-mail your friends, call your loved ones, and write the president—tell them all about the Manga Revolution!

And make sure you log on to **www.TOKYOPOP.com** for more manga!

WHEN AMANDA *FINALLY* GETS THE PET THAT SHE'S ALWAYS WANTED, THERE'S JUST ONE PROBLEM: SHE AND PEACH DON'T EXACTLY SEE EYE TO EYE! *PEACH FUZZ* SHOWS US THAT ALL FRIENDS CAN BE HARD TO UNDERSTAND... ESPECIALLY FURRY ONES WITH SHARP TEETH!

Peach Fuzz

FROM THE GRAND PRIZE WINNERS OF TOKYOPOP'S SECOND *RISING STARS OF MANGA* COMPETITION.

TOKYOPOP
SHE'S AN ARTIST WHO LIVES TO PAINT
HE'S A VAMPIRE WHO MODELS TO LIVE
MODEL™
AVAILABLE NOW
T
TEEN
AGE 13+
© 2001 Lee So-young All Rights Reserved.
www.TOKYOPOP.co